THE 2025
LENTEN
COMPANION

A DEVOTIONAL JOURNEY OF REFLECTION AND RENEWAL

Strengthening Faith on the Path to Easter

THOMAS KNIGHT

Chapter Zero LLC
16192 Coastal Highway
Lewes, 19958, Delaware – USA
Contact: info@chapterzerobooks.com

ISBN Paperback: 978-1-961963-52-8
ISBN Hardback: 978-1-961963-53-5

Contents

Introduction

Gracious and Loving God, as we stand on the threshold of Lent, we pause to acknowledge Your presence in this journey we are about to undertake. May this season be a time of deeper reflection, sincere repentance, and joyful anticipation of the Resurrection. Open our hearts to the transformative power of Your love as we walk these forty days with Christ. Amen.

Dear Reader,

Welcome to a journey of the heart. Your decision to walk through this Lenten season with intention and reflection is a powerful step toward deeper communion with God. This book serves both as an invitation and a guide—a companion for the days ahead as we strive to draw closer to God's heart. Together, let us embark on this sacred path, rediscovering the depths of God's love and the richness of His grace in our lives.

This book is designed to be your daily guide from Ash Wednesday to Easter Sunday, crafted to deepen your relationship with God through scripture, reflection, prayer, and action. Each day offers a scripture passage, a meditation to ponder, a prayer to bring us closer to God, and a practical action step to live out our faith.

Through these pages, I hope you encounter God in both stillness and storm, in moments of joy and times of sorrow. This journey is about transformation—allowing God to reshape our hearts, renew our minds, and guide our steps. Whether this is your first Lenten journey or your fortieth, may this book be a source of comfort, challenge, and inspiration as we journey toward the cross and the glorious Resurrection that awaits.

Within these pages, you will find a daily structure designed to deepen your Lenten journey, including:

- **Scripture Reading**: A selected passage that grounds us in God's Word, reflecting the themes of repentance, reflection, sacrifice, and renewal that mark Lent.

- **Reflection**: Thoughtful meditations drawn from the day's scripture, offering insights and challenges to consider.

- **Action Step**: Practical suggestions to live out the day's theme, fostering active faith and spiritual discipline.

- **Prayer**: A concluding prayer for each devotion, centering our thoughts on God and seeking His guidance and strength.

Additionally, you will encounter weekly themes exploring different aspects of the Lenten experience, questions for journaling to facilitate personal reflection, and spaces for your own notes and prayers, making this journey uniquely yours.

To fully embrace the Lenten journey this companion offers:

1. **Set Aside Time**: Choose a consistent time each day for your reading and reflection, whether morning, midday, or evening. Consistency is key to transformative power.

2. **Create a Sacred Space**: Find a quiet, comfortable spot where you can be undisturbed. This physical space can foster an internal space of contemplation and prayer.

3. **Keep a Journal**: Recording your thoughts, prayers, and insights can enhance your reflection and provide a record of your spiritual journey through Lent.

4. Open Heart and Mind: Approach each day's reading with expectancy and openness, ready to hear what God might speak into your life.

While Lent is a time for personal reflection and repentance, it is also a collective journey we undertake as the body of Christ. You are invited to journey not only with the saints of ages past but also with a global community of believers, all seeking to draw closer to Christ. Share your insights, struggles, and victories with others, knowing that we are companions on the same path, walking with Christ toward the cross and the joy of Easter morning.

In faith,

Thomas Knight

Living Lent
Insights for Personal and Family Devotion

Understanding Lent

Lent is a solemn forty-day period in the Christian liturgical calendar, traditionally observed as a time of preparation for Easter. Starting on Ash Wednesday and concluding on Holy Saturday, Lent invites believers into a journey of reflection, repentance, and spiritual renewal. This season mirrors Jesus' forty days in the wilderness, offering us a space to deepen our relationship with God, reflect on our lives, and prepare our hearts for the celebration of Christ's resurrection.

The pillars of the Lenten observance—prayer, fasting, and almsgiving—are practices rooted in Scripture and upheld by Christians throughout the centuries. Each discipline serves a specific purpose in our spiritual growth and preparation:

- **Prayer** is the foundation of Lenten practice, providing a direct line of communication with God. It is a time to deepen our dialogue with the Divine, offering thanks, seeking forgiveness, and asking for guidance. Through prayer, we foster a posture of openness to God's will and a deeper awareness of His presence in our lives.

- **Fasting** involves the voluntary abstinence from certain foods, activities, or pleasures. It teaches self-discipline, helps purify our bodies and souls, and expresses our hunger for God. Fasting during Lent symbolically participates in Jesus' suffering and acknowledges our dependence on God for sustenance.

- **Almsgiving** reflects our call to love and serve others, extending generosity and compassion to those in need. It represents our gratitude for God's blessings and underscores our responsibility to care for our neighbors. Through acts of charity and service, we embody Christ's love in the world.

Together, these practices help to strip away the distractions of daily life, focusing our hearts and minds on the fundamental truths of our faith. Lent is not merely a period of denial but a season of positive action: engaging more deeply with God, practicing discipline and self-control, and living out the command to love our neighbors as ourselves.

As we begin this journey, let us seize the opportunity for transformation, allowing the practices of prayer, fasting, and almsgiving to lead us toward a deeper understanding of our faith and a more intimate connection with God. In doing so, we prepare not only to commemorate the sorrow of Good Friday but also to celebrate the joy of Easter Sunday with renewed hearts and spirits.

Prayer: Deepening Your Relationship with God

Prayer is the lifeline of a Christian's relationship with God—a sacred conversation that nurtures our connection with the Divine. During Lent, we are encouraged to enrich this relationship through intentional prayer practices. Below are varied ways to enhance your prayer life during this reflective season:

Establish a Routine for Prayer

- Morning Devotion: Begin each day with a moment of prayer. Consider setting your alarm a few minutes earlier to enjoy the tranquility of the morning. Use this time to dedicate your day to God, seeking His guidance and protection.

- Evening Reflection: End your day with a prayerful review of your day's events, expressing gratitude and requesting peace for a restful night. This can include moments of confession and intercession for yourself and others.

Creating a dedicated prayer space at home can solidify this routine, turning a portion of your living area into a sacred spot that symbolizes the importance of these moments.

Incorporate Scripture into Your Daily Prayer

- Daily Bible Verse: Blend scripture with your prayers by including a daily devotional or following a Lent-specific Bible reading plan highlighting passages pertinent to the season.

- Lectio Divina: Engage with this timeless practice by selecting a scripture passage to read, meditate upon, pray over, and contemplate each day or week during Lent. This approach allows the words of the Bible to deeply influence your spiritual reflections.

Foster Family Prayer Practices

- Share Prayer Requests: Allocate time for family members to share their prayer needs, fostering a supportive environment that underscores the significance of each person's concerns.

- Pray the Rosary: For those who follow this tradition, the Rosary can be a profound communal prayer experience during Lent. Focus particularly on the Sorrowful Mysteries, which reflect on Jesus' passion and resurrection.

- Engage with Family Devotionals: Choose a Lenten family devotional that offers prayers, scripture readings, and questions for reflection. Establish a consistent time for your family to gather, read, and discuss insights and spiritual growth.

Through these practices, prayer becomes a personal journey and a communal experience that strengthens the faith of individuals and families alike.

Fasting: Sacrifice and Self-Discipline

Fasting is a time-honored discipline in the Lenten season, physically expressing spiritual desire and self-discipline. It's a practice that invites us to make space for God by removing what might distract us from His presence. Here's how to approach fasting in a way that enriches your spiritual journey:

Understand the Purpose of Fasting

Fasting is more than abstaining from food or drink; it's a sacrificial practice that directs our hunger and thirst toward God. It reminds us of our dependence on Him for all things and allows us to share in a small part of Christ's suffering. By fasting, we create physical reminders of our spiritual needs, turning our attention away from worldly satisfactions to find fulfillment in God.

Choosing What to Fast From

- Beyond Food: Consider fasting from activities or habits that consume excessive time or attention, such as social media, television, or unnecessary spending. The goal is to free up space and time for prayer, reflection, and serving others.

- Technology Fast: Given the pervasive role of technology in our lives, a fast from social media or limiting screen time can be particularly meaningful, helping to quiet the noise that distracts from introspection and prayer.

- Simplifying Your Lifestyle: Fasting from unnecessary spending or luxury items can foster a spirit of simplicity and gratitude, making us more aware of the needs of others.

Fasting with Children

Children should be introduced to fasting with care, focusing on the concept of giving up something to make more room for Jesus in their lives.

- Simple Sacrifices: Encourage children to choose something meaningful to give up, such as a favorite snack, video games, or TV time, explaining how this can help them think about Jesus and others more.

- Positive Actions: Pair fasting with positive actions, like saving money not spent on treats to donate to charity or using time not spent on screens to read Bible stories together.

Balancing Health and Fasting

While fasting is a powerful spiritual discipline, it's essential to approach it in a way that does not harm your health.

- Listen to Your Body: Ensure that any fast you undertake is physically safe. This is particularly important for those with health conditions, pregnant women, or anyone for whom fasting from food might be inadvisable.

- Moderation and Mindfulness: Fasting should be challenging but not harmful. Consider partial fasts, such as skipping one meal a day or giving up certain types of food rather than all food.

- Stay Hydrated: Regardless of the type of fast, maintaining hydration is crucial. Even while abstaining from food, it is recommended to continue drinking water to support your health.

Fasting during Lent is an invitation to realign our hearts and priorities with God's. Whether through abstaining from certain foods or other forms of fasting, this discipline can lead to deeper spiritual insights and growth, drawing us closer to the heart of God and the true meaning of this sacred season.

Almsgiving: Extending Compassion and Generosity

Almsgiving is a fundamental aspect of the Lenten season, emphasizing the importance of extending compassion and generosity towards others. It's an expression of our gratitude for all that God has given us and a tangible way to participate in His work of caring for the needy. Here's how to incorporate almsgiving into your Lenten practice:

Identify Causes or Organizations to Support

- **Research and Selection:** Spend time researching charities or community projects that align with your values or those that directly impact your community. Look for organizations with transparent operations and a proven track record of making a difference.

- **Diverse Causes:** Consider a range of causes, including local food banks, international relief organizations, shelters for the homeless, and initiatives supporting education for underprivileged children.

Almsgiving as a Family

- **Involving Children:** Engage your children in the process of choosing a charity or community project to support. Discuss the importance of helping others and how even small contributions can make a big difference.

- **Service Projects:** Participate in or organize service projects appropriate for family involvement. This could be anything from volunteering at a local shelter to organizing a neighborhood clean-up.

Creative Ways to Give

- **Beyond Monetary Donations:** Look for opportunities to donate your time and skills. Volunteering at local charities, offering professional services pro bono, or teaching a skill you possess can be invaluable contributions.

- **Crafting for a Cause:** Engage in activities such as knitting, sewing, or crafting items to donate to hospitals, nursing homes, or shelters. This can be a meaningful way to give, allowing personal or family participation in creating the gifts.

Reflecting on the Impact

- **Family or Individual Reflection:** After participating in almsgiving, take time to reflect as a family or individually on the experience. Discuss the impact your contribution may have on others and how giving has influenced your spiritual journey.

- **Gratitude and Growth:** Use these reflections to cultivate a sense of gratitude for what you have and to recognize the growth in empathy and compassion within yourself and your family members.

Almsgiving during Lent is not just about giving from our abundance but about sharing in Christ's very love and compassion. It calls us to look beyond our needs and comforts to see the face of Christ in those we serve.

Other Lenten Commitments: Broadening Your Observance

Lent offers a rich tapestry of practices beyond prayer, fasting, and almsgiving, inviting us to explore a variety of commitments that can enhance our spiritual journey. Here are additional ways to deepen your Lenten observance and connect more meaningfully with this sacred season:

Attend Lenten Services

- **Ash Wednesday:** Begin Lent by attending an Ash Wednesday service, where ashes are placed on your forehead as a sign of repentance and mortality. This powerful symbol sets the tone for the season of reflection that follows.

- **Stations of the Cross:** Participate in the Stations of the Cross, a devotion that commemorates Jesus' last day on Earth. This practice is especially poignant during Lent, offering a way to meditate on Christ's sacrifices.

- **Special Lenten Services:** Many churches offer additional services during Lent, such as weekly prayer meetings or vespers. Attending these can provide structure to your Lenten journey and opportunities for communal worship.

Engage in Acts of Kindness

Consider making a conscious decision to perform acts of kindness throughout Lent. Engaging in daily encouragements or setting a goal for weekly gestures of generosity can significantly embody the love of Christ in tangible ways. Additionally, challenge yourself and your family to spontaneous acts of kindness. Simple actions such as writing a note of appreciation, paying for someone's coffee, or helping a neighbor can profoundly impact both the giver and the receiver.

Create a Lenten Calendar

Design a Lenten calendar to mark your spiritual growth with specific goals, scripture readings, or daily activities. This visual aid serves as a continual reminder of your commitments and progress. Encourage family involvement by having each member contribute ideas for the calendar, transforming it into a collective spiritual journey that everyone can share and reflect upon together.

Lenten Crafts and Projects

Participate in reflective crafts to focus your thoughts on the themes of Lent. Consider making a prayer jar to collect prayers throughout the season or crafting a cross from natural materials. These activities can provide a meditative focus during Lent. Additionally, undertake family projects such as creating a

Lenten wreath or assembling a resurrection garden. These crafts do not only bring aesthetic value to your home but also act as visual reminders of the season's deeper meanings.

Incorporating these additional practices into your observance of Lent can enhance your spiritual journey, offering fresh avenues to embrace the season's invitation for reflection, repentance, and renewal.

Making Lent Meaningful

The true goal of this season is to draw closer to God and prepare our hearts for the profound celebration of Easter. I invite you, individually and as families, to reflect on your Lenten journey—consider how it has deepened your faith and brought you closer to the divine mystery we are about to celebrate. Remember, the path to Easter is as personal as it is sacred, offering each of us unique insights and opportunities for spiritual growth.

As we approach this time with open hearts, let us be prepared to be transformed by God's enduring love and grace. In the words of the Apostle Paul: "And do not be conformed to this world, but be transformed by the renewing of your mind, that you may prove what is that good and acceptable and perfect will of God" (Romans 12:2). This Lent, let us embrace the renewal of our minds and spirits, allowing God's transformative power to prepare us for the joy of Easter.

This Lent, let us embrace the renewal of our minds and spirits, allowing God's transformative power to prepare us for the joy of Easter.

Ash Wednesday, March 5
Awakening to Grace: Ash Wednesday Reflection

Heavenly Father, as we step into this sacred season of Lent, guide our hearts to truly awaken to Your grace. Help us see the path You have set before us with clear eyes and open hearts. Amen.

Scripture Reading:

Joel 2:12-13

"Yet even now," declares the Lord, "return to me with all your heart, with fasting, with weeping, and with mourning; and rend your hearts and not your garments." Return to the Lord your God, for he is gracious and merciful, slow to anger, and abounding in steadfast love; and he relents over disaster."

Reflection:

Ash Wednesday marks the beginning of our Lenten journey—a time to return to God wholeheartedly. Today, we stand at the threshold of a deeply personal spiritual voyage, an opportunity to delve into the depths of our souls and discover the grace that God freely offers. It's a day of contemplation, of recognizing our human frailty and our need for God's mercy. The ashes we receive are not just a symbol of penitence but a reminder of the grace that covers us and transforms our very being.

As you reflect on today's scripture, consider the areas of your life where you yearn for renewal and divine intervention. How can you open your heart more fully to the transformative power of God's grace this Lent?

Action Step:

Take a moment to write down one area of your life where you feel distant from God's grace. It could be a personal struggle, a relationship, or an aspect of your faith life that feels dry. Commit to bringing this area before God in prayer throughout Lent, asking for the grace to heal, renew, and transform.

Gracious God, as we begin this journey of Lent, we ask for the courage to return to You with all our hearts. May the ashes we receive today remind us of our need for Your grace and the renewal it brings. Help us to embrace this holy season with a spirit of humility and readiness to be transformed by Your love. Amen.

Thursday, March 6

Surrendering to Silence: Discovering Inner Peace

Lord of Peace, in the quiet of this day, help us to lay down the noise of our lives to discover the tranquility of Your presence. Teach us the power of surrendering to silence, where Your voice becomes clear. Amen.

Scripture Reading:

Psalm 46:10

"Be still, and know that I am God. I will be exalted among the nations, I will be exalted in the earth!"

Reflection:

In our bustling world, silence is a rare sanctuary. Yet, it is in these quiet moments that we can truly encounter the Divine. Today, we are called to surrender—not as a sign of defeat, but as an opening to peace and deeper understanding. To "be still" is to let go of our own agendas, fears, and distractions, allowing

God's voice to rise above the rest. It's an invitation to deepen our relationship with the Lord, recognizing His sovereignty and our place in His creation.

Reflect on the places and times when you have felt closest to God. Were these moments filled with noise and activity, or were they marked by stillness and peace? How can you create more space for silence in your daily life, to listen more intently to God's voice?

Action Step:

Today, dedicate at least 5 minutes to sit in silence. Find a quiet space where you won't be disturbed. Close your eyes, take deep breaths, and simply be present. If your mind wanders, gently bring your focus back to your breathing and God's peaceful presence. Consider making this practice a daily habit during Lent.

God of Stillness, in the silence of this day, we seek Your face. Quiet our minds, still our hearts, and help us to hear Your gentle whisper above the clamor of our lives. May this practice of surrendering to silence draw us closer to You, finding peace in Your presence. Amen.

Friday, March 7

Solitude and Spirit: Finding God in Quiet

Gracious God, guide us into the solitude where we can meet You without distractions. In these moments of quiet, let our spirits be refreshed, and our connection with You deepened. Amen.

Scripture Reading:

Matthew 6:6

"But when you pray, go into your room, close the door, and pray to your Father, who is unseen. Then your Father, who sees what is done in secret, will reward you."

Reflection:

Solitude offers a sacred space for personal encounters with the Divine. Jesus Himself sought solitude to connect with the Father, teaching us the value of withdrawing from the world to engage in intimate conversation with God. In today's fast-paced environment, finding solitude can seem challenging, yet it is essential for our spiritual health. It allows us to shed the roles and expectations that define us in the public eye, presenting our true selves before God.

Consider the barriers that prevent you from seeking solitude. Is it the fear of being alone with your thoughts, the discomfort of silence, or the constant demands of daily life? Reflect on how you can overcome these barriers to create meaningful spaces of solitude, even if it's just for a few moments each day.

Action Step:

Identify a specific time and place where you can be alone with God daily. It might be a quiet corner of your home, a park bench, or even a secluded spot during your daily walk. Commit to spending this time in solitude, bringing your thoughts, prayers, and questions to God. Use this time not just for speaking but also for listening, allowing God's spirit to speak to your heart.

Dear Lord, in the solitude of our hearts, we seek Your presence. Help us to find the quiet spaces where we can be alone with You, to hear Your voice and feel Your love. May these moments of solitude strengthen our faith and renew our spirits. In Your holy name, we pray. Amen.

Saturday, March 8
The Gift of Patience: Embracing God's Timing

Lord of Time and Eternity, teach us to embrace the gift of patience as we learn to trust in Your timing. Guide our hearts to find peace in the waiting, knowing that You are with us in every moment. Amen.

⸺◆◇◆⸺

Scripture Reading:

James 1:4

"Let perseverance finish its work so that you may be mature and complete, not lacking anything."

⸺◆◇◆⸺

Reflection:

Patience is more than just waiting; it's an active trust in God's plan for our lives. In our journey of faith, we often encounter situations that test our patience and challenge our ability to trust in God's timing. These moments, though difficult, are growth opportunities. They mold us into "mature and complete" individuals, as James writes. Today, reflect on the areas of your life where you are being called to practice patience. Is it in a personal goal, a relationship, or a deeper spiritual understanding?

Consider how embracing patience can transform your perspective on these challenges. Instead of viewing delays or obstacles as hindrances, see them as moments prepared by God for your growth and preparation.

Action Step:

Identify one situation in your life where impatience has taken root. Commit to offering this situation to God in prayer, asking for the patience to wait on His timing. Each time you find yourself growing impatient, pause to remind yourself of God's faithfulness and His perfect timing. Reflect on how this practice of patience might be shaping you for what lies ahead.

Patient Father, in our haste, we often forget the wisdom of Your timing. Help us see the value in waiting and trust in Your plan for our lives. May the gift of patience lead us to a deeper understanding of Your love and purpose for us. In Jesus' name, we pray. Amen.

Sunday, March 9
Sabbath Rest and Reflection: Honoring God's Rhythm

Lord of the Sabbath, grant us the wisdom to embrace Your rhythm of rest and work. Teach us to honor the Sabbath not just as a day of obligation but as a gift for our well-being and spiritual renewal. Amen.

Scripture Reading:

Mark 2:27

"Then he said to them, 'The Sabbath was made for man, not man for the Sabbath.'"

Reflection:

In a culture that often celebrates busyness and productivity, the concept of Sabbath rest can seem counterintuitive. Yet, Jesus reminds us that the Sabbath is a gift from God, designed for our benefit. It's a time to pause from our labor, to reflect on God's goodness, and to rejuvenate our bodies and spirits. The Sabbath offers us a chance to reset our priorities, placing God and our wellbeing at the center of our lives once again.

Reflect on how you currently observe the Sabbath. Does it feel like a day of rest and connection with God, or has it become just another busy day? What changes can you make to reclaim the Sabbath as a time of rest, worship, and family?

Action Step:

Today, commit to a Sabbath observance that refreshes your spirit and honors God. Plan restorative and life-giving activities, whether attending a worship service, spending time in nature, reading scripture, or enjoying unhurried time with loved ones. Avoid tasks that drain your energy or pull your focus away from God. Let this Sabbath be a true rest in God's presence.

Heavenly Father, thank You for the gift of the Sabbath, a weekly reminder of Your care for us. Help us embrace this day of rest as an opportunity to draw closer to You and to recharge our bodies and souls. May we find joy in the Sabbath, recognizing it as a sacred time set apart for Your glory and our renewal. In Jesus' name, Amen.

Monday, March 10

Finding Peace in Prayer: Connecting with God's Heart

Creator of Peace, draw us closer to the heart of Your love through prayer. As we seek Your face, grant us the peace that transcends understanding, anchoring us in Your presence. Amen.

Scripture Reading:

Philippians 4:6-7

"Do not be anxious about anything, but in every situation, by prayer and petition, with thanksgiving, present your requests to God. And the peace of God, which transcends all understanding, will guard your hearts and your minds in Christ Jesus."

Reflection:

Finding true peace can seem elusive in a world filled with turmoil and uncertainty. Yet, the Apostle Paul directs us to the source of all peace—prayer. Through prayer, we open our hearts to God, sharing our deepest concerns, fears, and desires. In these moments of vulnerability and trust, we connect most profoundly with God's heart, allowing His peace to envelop us.

Reflect today on the nature of your prayer life. Is it a one-sided conversation, or do you allow space to listen, to truly hear what God might be speaking into your life? Consider how shifting towards a more dialogical approach to prayer could deepen your sense of peace and connection with God.

Action Step:

Today, dedicate a portion of your prayer time to simply listening. After presenting your requests to God, sit in silence for a few minutes. Keep a journal nearby to write down any thoughts, impressions, or feelings that come to you during this time. This practice may feel challenging at first, but it can become a powerful way to experience God's peace and guidance.

Lord of all Peace, thank You for the gift of prayer, a sacred connection that brings us into Your presence. Help us find peace in these moments of communion with You, trusting that You are always listening, speaking, and present. May our hearts be open to receive the peace You generously offer. In Jesus' name, Amen.

Tuesday, March 11
Cultivating Compassion: Living Out God's Love

Compassionate Father, help us to embody Your love in our actions and attitudes. Teach us to see others through Your eyes, extending compassion and kindness to all we meet. Amen.

Scripture Reading:

Colossians 3:12

"Therefore, as God's chosen people, holy and dearly loved, clothe yourselves with compassion, kindness, humility, gentleness, and patience."

Reflection:

Compassion is at the heart of Jesus's teachings and life. It's an active desire to alleviate the suffering of others, a reflection of God's boundless love for us. In a world that often values individualism and self-sufficiency, choosing to live compassionately is a powerful testimony of our faith. It requires us to look beyond our own needs and desires, be present with those suffering, and take action in whatever ways we can to help.

Today, consider how you can clothe yourself with compassion. Are there individuals in your community who are overlooked or in need? How can you extend God's love to them, not just in words, but in tangible acts of kindness and support?

Action Step:

Identify one practical act of compassion you can perform today. It might be reaching out to someone who is lonely, volunteering your time for a cause, or simply offering a kind word to a stranger. Make a commitment to carry out this act, keeping your heart open to any other opportunities God may present for you to show compassion.

Lord of Love, thank You for showing us the ultimate example of compassion through Your Son, Jesus Christ. Inspire us to follow in His footsteps, seeking out and responding to the needs of those around us. May our lives reflect Your love and compassion to the world. In Jesus' name, we pray. Amen.

Wednesday, March 12
The Journey of Forgiveness: Healing Through God's Grace

Merciful God, open our hearts to the power of forgiveness. Help us to release the burdens of resentment and embrace the freedom and healing that comes from Your grace. Amen.

Scripture Reading:

Ephesians 4:31-32

"Get rid of all bitterness, rage and anger, brawling and slander, along with every form of malice. Be kind and compassionate to one another, forgiving each other, just as in Christ God forgave you."

Reflection:

Forgiveness is a cornerstone of the Christian faith, not merely a suggestion but a command that reflects the very essence of God's nature. It is both a gift we receive and a gift we are called to give. The journey of forgiveness can be challenging, especially when the wounds are deep. Yet, it is essential for our spiritual health and our relationships. Forgiveness frees us from the chains of bitterness and opens the path to reconciliation and peace.

Today, reflect on any areas of unforgiveness in your life. How might holding onto bitterness be affecting your relationship with God and others? Consider the freedom that could come from letting go and allowing God's grace to heal your heart.

Action Step:

Identify someone you need to forgive or seek forgiveness from. Begin this process through prayer, asking God for the courage and humility to forgive or to ask for forgiveness. If you're ready, take the next step to communicate this forgiveness or apology, whether through a letter, a call, or in person, guided by wisdom and love.

Gracious Father, thank You for the incredible gift of forgiveness that You freely offer us through Jesus Christ. Grant us the strength to forgive others as You have forgiven us. May our hearts be healed and our relationships restored by Your boundless grace and mercy. In Jesus' name, we pray. Amen.

Thursday, March 13

Overcoming Temptation: Strengthened by Faith

Almighty God, who faced temptation and overcame it, fortify us with Your strength. Guide us to stand firm in faith when faced with trials and temptations, relying on Your word and Spirit. Amen.

Scripture Reading:

1 Corinthians 10:13

"No temptation has overtaken you except what is common to mankind. And God is faithful; he will not let you be tempted beyond what you can bear. But when you are tempted, he will also provide a way out so that you can endure it."

Reflection:

Temptation is a universal experience, yet it often makes us feel isolated in our struggle. The Apostle Paul reassures us that we are not alone in facing temptation or overcoming it. God's faithfulness is our shield, and His grace, our strength. This verse not only acknowledges the reality of temptation but also promises divine assistance to find a way through it.

Reflect on the temptations that challenge you most deeply. How do they test your faith? How can you seek God's guidance and strength in those moments? Remember, overcoming temptation is not about relying on our own willpower but on drawing closer to God and His infinite resources.

Action Step:

Today, identify a specific temptation you are facing. Make a plan for how you will seek God's help the next time this temptation arises. This could involve memorizing a Scripture verse to counteract the temptation, finding a prayer partner to call for support, or removing yourself from situations that typically lead to temptation. Trust in God's promise to provide a way out.

Lord of Strength and Mercy, thank You for Your promise to be with us in our moments of temptation. Help us to rely on Your power and not our own, to seek Your way out in times of trial. May our victories over temptation draw us closer to You and strengthen our faith. In Jesus' name, we pray. Amen.

Friday, March 14
The Grace of Humility: Walking in Jesus' Footsteps

Lord Jesus, who exemplified humility in Your life and teachings, mold our hearts to mirror Your humility. Help us to walk in Your footsteps, putting others before ourselves and recognizing our need for Your grace. Amen.

Scripture Reading:

Philippians 2:3-4

"Do nothing out of selfish ambition or vain conceit. Rather, in humility value others above yourselves, not looking to your own interests but each of you to the interests of the others."

Reflection:

Humility is a foundational Christian virtue, yet often misunderstood. It is not thinking less of ourselves but thinking of ourselves less, focusing on how we can serve and uplift others. Jesus Christ is our ultimate model of humility, from

His incarnation to His selfless acts of washing the disciples' feet and sacrificing His life for us. In today's fast-paced, self-centered world, embracing humility as Jesus did is a radical act of faith and obedience.

Consider areas in your life where pride might be overshadowing humility. How can adopting a posture of humility enhance your relationships, your work, and your spiritual journey? Reflect on how you can serve others today in a way that reflects Jesus' humility.

Action Step:

Choose one practical act of service you can perform today without seeking recognition or reward. It might be something as simple as lending a listening ear, offering to help a colleague or neighbor, or performing a random act of kindness. As you do this, keep your focus on the joy of serving rather than on the outcome or acknowledgment.

Heavenly Father, thank You for the perfect example of humility shown through Your Son, Jesus Christ. Guide us to embrace and practice humility in our daily lives, serving others selflessly and walking in the path that Jesus laid out for us. May our lives reflect His love and humility to all we encounter. Amen.

Saturday, March 15
Listening for God's Voice: The Path to Spiritual Clarity

Loving God, who speaks in the stillness and in the storm, tune our hearts to Your voice. Help us distinguish Your guidance from the world's noise, leading us to deeper understanding and clarity. Amen.

Scripture Reading:

1 Kings 19:11-12

"The Lord said, 'Go out and stand on the mountain in the presence of the Lord, for the Lord is about to pass by.' Then a great and powerful wind tore the mountains apart and shattered the rocks before the Lord, but the Lord was not in the wind. After the wind, there was an earthquake, but the Lord was not in the earthquake. After the earthquake came a fire, but the Lord was not in the fire. And after the fire came a gentle whisper."

Reflection:

In a world brimming with constant communication and distractions, listening to God's voice can seem like a daunting task. Yet, the story of Elijah reminds us that God often speaks in the unexpected—in a gentle whisper rather than the tumult of our surroundings. This passage invites us to seek God in the quiet, to cultivate a practice of listening that goes beyond our ears to our hearts.

Consider the ways you have sought to hear God's voice. Can you adopt practices or habits to better attune yourself to the divine whispers in your life? How might creating spaces of silence and reflection in your daily routine enhance your ability to listen?

Action Step:

Commit to a daily quiet time dedicated solely to listening for God's voice. This could involve meditative reading of the Scriptures, sitting in silence, or journaling. The goal is not to fill the time with your words but to allow space for God to speak into your life. Note any thoughts, feelings, or impressions you receive during this time.

God of Whispers, thank You for Your promise to speak into our lives. Grant us the patience and discernment to listen for Your gentle voice amidst the clamor of our daily existence. May we find spiritual clarity and direction as we learn to listen more deeply. In Your holy name, we pray. Amen.

Sunday, March 16
Acts of Kindness: Extending God's Love in Practical Ways

Gracious God, whose love is boundless and unconditional, inspire us to extend Your love through acts of kindness today. Help us to be vessels of Your grace, touching the lives of others with the warmth of Your compassion. Amen.

Scripture Reading:

Galatians 5:22-23

"But the fruit of the Spirit is love, joy, peace, patience, kindness, goodness, faithfulness, gentleness, and self-control. Against such things, there is no law."

Reflection:

Kindness is a powerful expression of God's character and a tangible way we can demonstrate His love to the world. It transcends words, impacting the hearts of both the giver and receiver. In a society often marked by indifference and hostility, a simple act of kindness can be a beacon of hope and a testament to the transformative power of God's love.

Reflect on the last time you were on the receiving end of an act of kindness. How did it make you feel? Now, consider how you can be a conduit of God's kindness today. It doesn't have to be grandiose; even the smallest gesture can significantly impact someone's life.

Action Step:

Identify one act of kindness you can perform today. It could be as simple as sending an encouraging message, helping a neighbor, or sharing a smile with a stranger. Make a conscious effort to look for opportunities to show kindness throughout your day, keeping in mind that these acts are an extension of God's love.

Lord of Love and Kindness, thank You for the countless ways You show Your love to us each day. Empower us to spread Your love through our actions, making kindness a hallmark of our lives. May each act of kindness we perform bring glory to Your name and draw others closer to You. Amen.

Monday, March 17
The Strength of Faith: Anchored in Hope

Faithful God, strengthen our faith that it may be the anchor in our lives, holding us steadfast in hope through every storm. Illuminate our path with Your truth, and guide us in unwavering trust in You. Amen.

——◆◇◆——

Scripture Reading:

Hebrews 11:1

"Now faith is confidence in what we hope for and assurance about what we do not see."

Reflection:

Faith is not merely belief; it is trust in action, a profound confidence in God's promises even when they are not yet visible on the horizon. This faith has empowered believers throughout the ages to face challenges with courage and hold on to hope in the darkest times. Faith acts as an anchor, keeping us grounded in God's truth and love, ensuring that the currents of doubt and fear do not sweep us away.

Reflect on the role of faith in your life. How has your faith been tested, and how has it grown as a result? Consider the ways in which a stronger faith could transform your outlook on life's challenges, imbuing you with a deeper sense of hope and purpose.

Action Step:

Identify one area of your life where you feel uncertainty or fear. Commit to exercising your faith in this area by taking a tangible step of trust. This could involve making a decision you've been postponing, starting a new venture, or simply dedicating your worries to God in prayer, trusting in His guidance and provision.

Lord of Hope, thank You for the gift of faith, which lights our way and anchors us in Your promises. Help us to cultivate a faith that is active and alive, a faith that endures trials and emerges stronger. May our lives be a testament to the strength that faith in You provides, drawing others to Your eternal hope. In Jesus' name, we pray. Amen.

Tuesday, March 18
Reflecting on Sacrifice: Embracing the Cross

Heavenly Father, as we reflect on the profound sacrifice of Your Son, Jesus Christ, on the cross, open our hearts to the depth of Your love and the magnitude of His sacrifice. Teach us to embrace the cross in our lives, recognizing it as the path to true freedom and salvation. Amen.

Scripture Reading:

Romans 5:8

"But God demonstrates His own love for us in this: While we were still sinners, Christ died for us."

Reflection:

The cross is the ultimate symbol of love and sacrifice in the Christian faith. It reminds us that before we ever sought God, He reached out to us with an act of incomparable love. This sacrifice is the foundation of our salvation and a call to carry our crosses daily. To embrace the cross is to accept the challenges and sacrifices that come with following Christ, knowing that through them, we are drawn closer to Him and transformed into His likeness.

Consider what the cross means in your life. Are there areas where God calls you to accept sacrifice or lay down your desires for the sake of others? How can reflecting on Jesus' sacrifice inspire you to live more selflessly and lovingly?

Action Step:

Identify one way you can embrace the spirit of sacrifice in your life today. This might involve giving up your time, resources, or personal preferences for the benefit of someone else. As you do this, reflect on the sacrifice Jesus made for you and consider how your actions, however small, can reflect His love for those around you.

Lord Jesus, thank You for the unmeasurable sacrifice of the cross, through which we have found life and salvation. Help us to carry our crosses with grace, following in Your footsteps of love and sacrifice. May our lives be a reflection of Your love for the world, drawing others closer to the heart of the gospel. In Your precious name, we pray. Amen.

Wednesday, March 19
The Call to Serve: Finding Joy in Selflessness

God of Service, who came not to be served but to serve, instill in us a heart that finds joy in serving others. Guide our actions to reflect Your selfless love, showing us the path to true fulfillment in giving of ourselves. Amen.

———◆O◆———

Scripture Reading:

Matthew 20:26-28

"It is not so among you, but whoever wishes to become great among you shall be your servant, and whoever wishes to be first among you shall be your slave; just as the Son of Man did not come to be served, but to serve, and to give His life a ransom for many."

———◆O◆———

Reflection:

In a world that often prioritizes personal gain and status, Jesus presents a radical counter-narrative: greatness in the Kingdom of God is measured by our willingness to serve. This call to service is not a burden but a source of joy and purpose, allowing us to partake in God's work in the world. Serving others enables us to break free from the confines of self-interest and discover the deep satisfaction that comes from self-giving love.

Reflect on your own life and community. Where is God calling you to serve? How can shifting your focus from being served to serving transform your relationships and your spiritual journey?

Action Step:

Identify a specific opportunity to serve in your community this week. It could be volunteering at a local charity, helping a neighbor in need, or offering your skills and time to your church or another organization. Approach this service with a prayerful heart, seeking to find joy and purpose in the act of giving yourself for the benefit of others.

Merciful God, thank You for the example of Your Son, who embodied the true essence of greatness through service. Help us to embrace this call to serve with joyful hearts, finding in it the path to true fulfillment. May our lives reflect Your love and generosity, inspiring a culture of service in Your name. Amen.

Thursday, March 20

Understanding Love: God's Unfailing Compassion

Eternal Love, from whom all love flows, deepen our understanding of Your unfailing compassion and teach us to love as You love, unconditionally and without reserve. Amen.

Scripture Reading:

1 John 4:7-8

"Dear friends, let us love one another, for love comes from God. Everyone who loves has been born of God and knows God. Whoever does not love does not know God, because God is love."

Reflection:

The essence of God's character is love—pure, unconditional, and all-encompassing. This divine love is the source from which all true love flows, calling us to love not just in words, but in action and truth. Understanding God's love transforms us, motivating us to extend that love to others, even when it's challenging. It's a reminder that to truly know God is to reflect His love in our daily lives.

Reflect on your experience of God's love. How has it shaped your interactions with others? Are there areas in your life where you struggle to show love? Consider how embracing God's model of love can break down barriers and heal relationships.

Action Step:

Today, make a conscious effort to show love in a practical way to someone who may be difficult to love. This could be through a kind gesture, a word of encouragement, or simply offering forgiveness where it's needed. As you do this, remember you're reflecting God's love, a love that knows no bounds.

God of Perfect Love, thank You for loving us with an everlasting love. Help us to grasp the breadth and depth of Your love more fully, that our lives might be a testament to Your compassion. Teach us to love as You love, breaking down walls and building bridges in Your name. Amen.

Friday, March 21
The Essence of Hope: Anchored in God's Promises

Lord of Hope, anchor our hearts in the certainty of Your promises. In a world that often feels uncertain, teach us to cling to the hope we have in You, transforming our perspective and guiding our steps. Amen.

———◆O◆———

Scripture Reading:

Hebrews 6:19

"We have this hope as an anchor for the soul, firm and secure. It enters the inner sanctuary behind the curtain."

———◆O◆———

Reflection:

Hope in the Christian context is not wishful thinking but a confident expectation based on the promises of God. It is an anchor for our souls, providing stability and security even in life's most tumultuous storms. This hope is rooted in the character of God and the fulfillment of His promises through Jesus Christ.

It invites us to look beyond our current circumstances to the eternal joy set before us.

Reflect on the areas of your life where hope feels dim. How can anchoring your hope in God's promises change your perspective on these situations? Consider the transformative power of hope—not just as a feeling but as a way of living that influences your decisions and interactions with others.

Action Step:

Identify a promise from Scripture that speaks to your current situation or a challenge you're facing. Commit this promise to memory, and each day this week, spend a few moments meditating on it. Allow this truth to renew your hope, reminding you of God's faithfulness and the future He has prepared for you.

Faithful God, thank You for the gift of hope, an anchor for our souls. In moments of doubt or despair, remind us of Your promises and the secure future we have in You. May our lives reflect the hope we possess, drawing others to seek the source of all hope. In Jesus' name, we pray. Amen.

Saturday, March 22
Walking with Trust: Navigating Life's Uncertainties

Sovereign Lord, in the midst of life's uncertainties, teach us to walk with trust in You. Guide our steps according to Your word, and help us lean not on our understanding but on Your unchanging love and wisdom. Amen.

Scripture Reading:

Proverbs 3:5-6

"Trust in the Lord with all your heart and lean not on your own understanding; in all your ways submit to Him, and He will make your paths straight."

Reflection:

Trust is foundational to our journey with God. It calls us to relinquish control, to surrender our plans and understanding in favor of God's perfect wisdom and timing. This can be especially challenging in moments of uncertainty when the way forward is unclear. Yet, in these moments, our trust is most profoundly tested and strengthened. By submitting our ways to God, we are promised guidance and clarity, not necessarily in the form of immediate answers, but as a path that leads us closer to Him and His purposes for our lives.

Consider the areas of your life where you struggle to trust God. What fears or doubts hold you back? Reflect on the peace and assurance that come from placing your trust in God, knowing that He is with you and for you, guiding you every step of the way.

Action Step:

Identify one decision or situation where you need to trust God more fully. Commit to praying about this situation every day for the next week, specifically asking God to increase your trust in Him and to show you the next step to take. Write down any insights or directions you receive, and be prepared to act in obedience, trusting in His guidance.

Lord of Wisdom, we thank You for Your promise to guide us when we place our trust in You. Help us to surrender our fears and doubts, choosing to walk in trust and obedience. May our lives be a testament to Your faithfulness, as we depend on You for every decision and challenge we face. In Jesus' name, we pray. Amen.

Sunday, March 23

The Practice of Gratitude: Cultivating a Thankful Heart

Creator of All Good Things, instill in us a spirit of gratitude for every blessing You bestow. Help us to recognize Your hand in all aspects of our lives, turning our hearts toward thanksgiving in all circumstances. Amen.

Scripture Reading:

1 Thessalonians 5:16-18

"Rejoice always, pray continually, give thanks in all circumstances; for this is God's will for you in Christ Jesus."

Reflection:

Gratitude is more than a feeling; it's a discipline that transforms our perspective, enabling us to see God's grace in every moment. This practice of thanksgiving doesn't ignore life's challenges but focuses on the abundance of God's blessings, enriching our faith and deepening our joy. In a world that often highlights what we lack, gratitude reminds us of the fullness of what we have in Christ.

Reflect on your current state of heart. Are there areas of your life where ingratitude has taken root, perhaps overshadowing God's gifts with discontent or envy? How can shifting your focus to gratitude change your attitude and actions?

Action Step:

Today, start a gratitude journal. Write down three things you're thankful for, and commit to adding to it daily. These can be as simple as the warmth of the sun, the support of a friend, or the provision of your daily needs. Make this practice a regular part of your prayer time, offering thanks to God for His unfailing love and the many ways He blesses you.

Gracious God, thank You for the countless gifts You generously pour into our lives. Teach us to cultivate a heart of gratitude, recognizing Your goodness at every turn. May this practice of thanksgiving draw us closer to You, filling our lives with joy and peace. In Jesus' name, we pray. Amen.

Monday, March 24
Seeking Wisdom: Guidance for Life's Journey

Wisdom-Giving God, illuminate our path with Your wisdom, guiding our decisions and directions according to Your will. Help us seek Your wisdom above all else, trusting it to lead us in the way of righteousness and peace. Amen.

Scripture Reading:

James 1:5

"If any of you lacks wisdom, let him ask God, who gives generously to all without reproach, and it will be given him."

Reflection:

In a world teeming with information and advice, discerning the right course of action can be daunting. Yet, the promise of James 1:5 stands as a beacon of hope: God freely offers wisdom to those who seek it earnestly. This divine wisdom is not merely intellectual knowledge but a profound understanding that shapes how we live, love, and interact with others. It's the wisdom that guides us to make choices that align with God's will, leading to life in its fullest.

Reflect on areas of your life where you need God's wisdom. Are you facing decisions or situations that seem beyond your understanding? How can you actively seek God's guidance in these moments, trusting Him to lead you?

Action Step:

Set aside time today to ask God for wisdom in a decision you are facing or a situation requiring discernment. Approach God with a humble and open heart, ready to listen and receive. Consider keeping a journal of these prayers and any insights or guidance you perceive, watching how God reveals His wisdom to you over time.

Lord of all Wisdom, we are grateful for Your promise to generously provide wisdom when we ask. Grant us the humility to seek Your guidance in every aspect of our lives, trusting in Your loving direction. May Your wisdom shape our paths, leading us to live in a manner worthy of Your calling. In Jesus' name, we pray. Amen.

Tuesday, March 25

Joy in the Journey: Celebrating God's Presence

Joyful God, who fills our lives with the richness of Your presence, help us to recognize and celebrate the joy found in walking with You every day. Ignite in our hearts a constant awareness of Your love, fueling our journey with unending joy. Amen.

Scripture Reading:

Psalm 16:11

"You make known to me the path of life; in Your presence there is fullness of joy; at Your right hand are pleasures forevermore."

Reflection:

Joy is not merely a fleeting emotion but a profound sense of well-being and contentment that comes from knowing we are in God's presence. It is a gift that transcends circumstances, rooted in the assurance of God's love and faithfulness. As we journey through life, with its highs and lows, the constant is God's presence, offering a deep and lasting joy that the world cannot give or take away.

Reflect on how you experience joy in your relationship with God. Are there practices or moments that particularly remind you of His presence and fill you with joy? How can you cultivate a lifestyle that is more attuned to the joy of walking with God daily?

Action Step:

Today, make a conscious effort to find joy in the simple moments of your day, recognizing them as gifts from God. It could be a moment of prayer, the beauty of nature, a kind interaction, or a passage of Scripture that speaks to you. Take a moment to thank God for these glimpses of joy, asking Him to help you become more aware of His presence in all aspects of your life.

Heavenly Father, thank You for the gift of Your presence, which brings fullness of joy into our lives. Help us to seek You and find You in every moment, celebrating the journey we share with You. May our hearts be ever joyful in Your love, spreading the light of Your joy to those around us. In Jesus' name, we pray. Amen.

Wednesday, March 26
The Path of Perseverance: Enduring Faith in Trials

Lord of Endurance, grant us the strength to persevere through every trial with unwavering faith. Teach us to see challenges as opportunities to grow closer to You and to strengthen our trust in Your sovereign plan. Amen.

————◆○◆————

Scripture Reading:

Romans 5:3-4

"Not only so, but we also glory in our sufferings, because we know that suffering produces perseverance; perseverance, character; and character, hope."

————◆○◆————

Reflection:

Perseverance is a key aspect of the Christian life, a testament to the power of faith in the face of adversity. The journey of faith is marked by seasons of hardship, but these are not without purpose. They are the very means by which God shapes our character, deepens our hope, and refines our faith. Through trials, we learn not only to endure but to find joy and growth in the midst of suffering, leaning ever more on God's strength and less on our own.

Consider the trials you are currently facing. How can you shift your perspective to see them as opportunities for growth in perseverance and faith? How might God be using these challenges to draw you closer to Him?

Action Step:

Identify one specific trial you are enduring. Commit to approaching it with a mindset of perseverance, seeking God's guidance and strength daily. Keep a journal of your journey through this trial, noting how your faith is being tested and strengthened, and how you see God working in the midst of it.

In the face of trials, Almighty God, we cling to You, the source of our strength and hope. Help us to persevere with a faith that is steadfast, trusting in Your good and perfect will for our lives. May we emerge from every challenge more refined, more hopeful, and more reliant on You. In Jesus' name, we pray. Amen.

Thursday, March 27

Embodying Christ's Love: A Call to Compassionate Action

Merciful Savior, who embodied perfect love and compassion, inspire us to follow in Your footsteps. Help us to see the world through Your eyes, acting with kindness and mercy that transcends our understanding. Amen.

———◆———

Scripture Reading:

Colossians 3:12-14

"Therefore, as God's chosen people, holy and dearly loved, clothe yourselves with compassion, kindness, humility, gentleness, and patience. Bear with each other and forgive one another if any of you has a grievance against someone. Forgive as the Lord forgave you. And over all these virtues put on love, which binds them all together in perfect unity."

———◆———

Reflection:

Embodying Christ's love is actively engaging in the world with a heart of compassion, kindness, humility, gentleness, and patience. It's a call to feel empathy and move towards others in tangible acts of love and service. This love is not passive; it seeks out the lost, comforts the hurting, and forgives the offender. In a world often divided by hatred and indifference, embodying Christ's love is a revolutionary act that can transform hearts and communities.

Reflect on how Christ's love has touched your life. How can you extend that same love to others? Are there specific individuals or groups whom God is calling you to serve with compassion and kindness?

Action Step:

Choose one action this week that reflects Christ's love in a practical way. It could be volunteering your time, reaching out to someone who is lonely, or offering forgiveness where there has been hurt. As you prepare for this act of love, pray for God to use you as an instrument of His peace and kindness.

Jesus, our model of perfect love, thank You for showing us what it means to love unconditionally. Empower us by Your Spirit to be Your hands and feet in this world, bringing light to dark places and hope to despairing hearts. May our lives reflect Your love in all we do, drawing others closer to You. Amen.

Friday, March 28
The Light of God's Presence: Illuminating Our Path

Lord of Light, in whom there is no darkness at all, illuminate our lives with the light of Your presence. Dispel the shadows of doubt and fear, guiding our steps along the path of righteousness and peace. Amen.

Scripture Reading:

Psalm 119:105

"Your word is a lamp for my feet, a light on my path."

Reflection:

In a world where uncertainty and darkness can cloud our way, the promise of God's word as a guiding light is a source of immense comfort and hope. God's presence illuminates our path, not always revealing the entire journey at once but providing enough light for the step we're on. This divine guidance is a call to trust, to walk in faith even when the way forward is not fully clear, confident that God is with us, leading us onward.

Reflect on how you have experienced the guiding light of God's presence in your life. Are there areas where you are currently seeking direction? How can you more fully rely on God's word as the lamp to your feet and the light to your path?

Action Step:

Commit to spending time in God's word daily, seeking His guidance and wisdom. Choose a specific scripture that speaks to your current situation or decision, and meditate on it throughout the week. Ask God to illuminate your path through His word, making clear the steps you are to take.

Heavenly Father, thank You for the gift of Your word, which lights our way and guides our steps. Help us to walk in the light of Your presence, trusting in Your wisdom and guidance. May we be beacons of Your light in the world, leading others to find their way to You. In Jesus' name, we pray. Amen.

Saturday, March 29
Renewal of Mind and Spirit: Embracing Transformation

Transforming God, who makes all things new, work within us to renew our minds and spirits. Help us to embrace the transformative power of Your Spirit, aligning our thoughts and actions with Your will. Amen.

———————◆◇◆———————

Scripture Reading:

Romans 12:2

"Do not conform to the pattern of this world, but be transformed by the renewing of your mind. Then you will be able to test and approve what God's will is—his good, pleasing and perfect will."

———————◆◇◆———————

Reflection:

In a culture that often promotes conformity and fleeting satisfactions, the call to be transformed by the renewing of our minds stands as a radical invitation to spiritual awakening. This renewal is not a one-time event but a continuous process of growth, requiring our active participation. By immersing ourselves in God's Word and being receptive to the Holy Spirit's guidance, we can begin to see the world through God's eyes, discerning His will and purpose for our lives.

Reflect on areas of your life that may need renewal. How can you open yourself more fully to God's transforming work? What practices can help you cultivate a mindset that seeks God's will above all else?

Action Step:

Identify one practical step you can take this week to foster renewal in your mind and spirit. It might be committing to a daily devotional time, engaging in a spiritual retreat, or seeking mentorship and accountability in your walk with God. Whatever you choose, let it be a step toward deeper transformation in Christ.

Lord of Transformation, thank You for the promise of renewal and growth in You. Guide us through the process of renewing our minds so that we may live lives that reflect Your truth and love. May we be ever open to the work of Your Spirit, transforming us into Your likeness day by day. Amen.

Sunday, March 30

The Peace of Forgiveness: Healing Broken Relationships

Healing God, who reconciles us to Yourself and one another, guide us in the path of forgiveness. Help us to release the burden of grudges and to embrace the peace that comes from reconciliation. Amen.

Scripture Reading:

Ephesians 4:31-32

"Get rid of all bitterness, rage and anger, brawling and slander, along with every form of malice. Be kind and compassionate to one another, forgiving each other, just as in Christ God forgave you."

Reflection:

Forgiveness is at the heart of the Gospel, a powerful act of grace that can transform lives and heal relationships. It's not always easy, especially when the wounds are deep, but it's a crucial step toward peace and healing. Forgiveness frees us from the chains of bitterness and anger, allowing us to move forward in love and compassion. It reflects God's forgiveness towards us, underscoring the importance of extending that same grace to others.

Reflect on the relationships in your life that may be strained by unforgiveness. What steps can you take toward healing and reconciliation? How can the act of forgiveness bring peace not only to your relationships but also to your own heart?

Action Step:

Choose one relationship that needs the healing touch of forgiveness. Pray for the strength and humility to initiate reconciliation, whether through a conversation, a letter, or a simple act of kindness. Remember, forgiveness is a process, and the first step can be the most challenging yet the most rewarding.

Merciful Father, thank You for the gift of Your forgiveness, which restores and renews us. Empower us to forgive as we have been forgiven, breaking down walls of bitterness and building bridges of peace. May our relationships reflect Your love and grace, healing wounds and uniting hearts. In Jesus' name, we pray. Amen.

Monday, March 31
Nurturing Spiritual Growth: Cultivating a Deeper Faith

Faithful Gardener, who nurtures our souls for growth, help us to cultivate a deeper, more vibrant faith. Guide our efforts to seek You, to understand Your Word, and to live out Your teachings in our daily lives. Amen.

Scripture Reading:

2 Peter 1:5-8

"For this very reason, make every effort to supplement your faith with virtue, and virtue with knowledge, and knowledge with self-control, and self-control with steadfastness, and steadfastness with godliness, and godliness with brotherly affection, and brotherly affection with love. For if these qualities are yours and are increasing, they keep you from being ineffective or unfruitful in the knowledge of our Lord Jesus Christ."

Reflection:

Spiritual growth is an intentional pursuit, akin to a gardener tending to a garden. It requires effort, patience, and the right conditions to flourish. Peter's exhortation to supplement faith with virtues such as knowledge, self-control, and love outlines a path for this growth. Each virtue builds upon the other, leading to a life that is fruitful and effective in the knowledge of Christ. This process of growth not only deepens our relationship with God but also enhances our witness to the world.

Reflect on your current spiritual practices. Are there areas where you feel called to grow? How can you intentionally nurture your faith, ensuring that it continues to deepen and mature?

Action Step:

Identify one spiritual discipline you would like to develop further, such as prayer, meditation on Scripture, fasting, or serving others. Commit to fully incorporating this discipline into your routine over the next month. Seek resources or guidance if necessary, and be mindful of the growth in your relationship with God as you deepen this practice.

Lord of All Growth, thank You for the invitation to grow in faith and virtue. Help us to be diligent in our pursuit of spiritual maturity, trusting that You will guide and enrich our efforts. May our lives bear the fruit of Your Spirit, showing the beauty and depth of a life rooted in You. Amen.

Tuesday, April 1
The Art of Letting Go: Trusting God with Our Burdens

Lord of Peace, who invites us to cast all our anxieties on You, help us to master the art of letting go. Teach us to trust You with our burdens, finding rest and freedom in Your care. Amen.

Scripture Reading:

1 Peter 5:7

"Cast all your anxiety on him because he cares for you."

Reflection:

Letting go is an act of trust, a surrender of our worries, fears, and burdens to God, who cares for us deeply. It challenges our desire to control and our tendency to cling to what burdens us, offering a path to peace and reliance on God's provision instead. This act of faith acknowledges God's sovereignty and His ability to bear what we cannot, leading us to a place of rest and security in His loving arms.

Reflect on the burdens you are holding onto. What fears or anxieties are you struggling to release? How can the practice of casting your cares on God change your perspective and lighten your load?

Action Step:

Identify a specific worry or burden that you need to let go of. Take a quiet moment to pray, physically opening your hands as a symbol of releasing this burden to God. Trust in His loving care and provision, and seek to maintain this posture of openness and trust as you move forward.

Compassionate Father, thank You for Your unfailing care and support. As we learn to let go of our burdens, fill us with Your peace and strength. May we walk in the freedom of Your love, trusting that You are more than capable of carrying our cares. In Jesus' name, we pray. Amen.

Wednesday, April 2

Finding Strength in Weakness: The Power of Vulnerability

Mighty God, in our moments of weakness, remind us of Your strength. Teach us the value of vulnerability, allowing Your power to be made perfect in our frailties. Guide us to embrace our limitations as opportunities for Your grace to shine. Amen.

<hr />

Scripture Reading:

2 Corinthians 12:9-10

"But he said to me, 'My grace is sufficient for you, for my power is made perfect in weakness.' Therefore I will boast all the more gladly about my weaknesses, so that Christ's power may rest on me. That is why, for Christ's sake, I delight in weaknesses, in insults, in hardships, in persecutions, in difficulties. For when I am weak, then I am strong."

<hr />

Reflection:

The world often tells us to hide our weaknesses, to present a facade of strength and self-sufficiency. However, the Christian journey invites us into a radical counter-narrative where our vulnerabilities are not sources of shame but of divine strength. Paul's revelation that God's power is made perfect in our weakness challenges us to rethink how we view our limitations. In acknowledging our weaknesses and relying on God's strength, we truly experience His power and grace in our lives.

Consider the areas of your life where you feel weakest. How can you offer these weaknesses to God, allowing His strength to be manifested in you? What does it mean for you to take delight in your weaknesses, as Paul did?

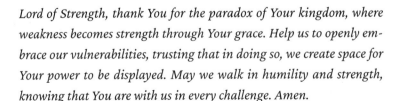

Action Step:

Reflect on a situation or aspect of your life where you feel vulnerable or weak. Commit to sharing this with a trusted friend, mentor, or prayer partner, asking for prayer and support. Through this act of vulnerability, observe how God's strength begins to work in and through you, transforming your perspective on weakness.

Lord of Strength, thank You for the paradox of Your kingdom, where weakness becomes strength through Your grace. Help us to openly embrace our vulnerabilities, trusting that in doing so, we create space for Your power to be displayed. May we walk in humility and strength, knowing that You are with us in every challenge. Amen.

Thursday, April 3
Celebrating Community: The Gift of Fellowship

God of Unity, who calls us into fellowship with one another, help us to celebrate the gift of community in our lives. Strengthen the bonds of friendship, family, and faith that connect us, and teach us to nurture these relationships with love and grace. Amen.

Scripture Reading:

Hebrews 10:24-25

"And let us consider how we may spur one another on toward love and good deeds, not giving up meeting together, as some are in the habit of doing, but encouraging one another—and all the more as you see the Day approaching."

Reflection:

Community is one of God's greatest gifts to us, a source of strength, encouragement, and love. In a culture that often glorifies individualism, the biblical call to live in fellowship with one another is a powerful reminder of our interconnectedness. Through community, we are called not only to support and uplift one another but also to spur each other on toward growth in love and good deeds. This mutual encouragement is vital to our spiritual health and to fulfilling our mission as followers of Christ.

Reflect on the role of community in your spiritual journey. How has fellowship with others encouraged or challenged you in your faith? In what ways can you contribute to building a stronger, more supportive community around you?

Action Step:

Identify one practical way you can strengthen the sense of community within your circle this week. It might be hosting a gathering, reaching out to someone who is isolated, or organizing a service project that brings people together for a common cause. Take the initiative to foster connections and celebrate the gift of fellowship.

Loving Father, thank You for the blessing of community and the joy of fellowship. Help us to be active participants in the body of Christ, nurturing the bonds that unite us and encouraging one another in faith and love. May our communities reflect Your love and grace to the world around us. In Jesus' name, we pray. Amen.

Friday, April 4
The Challenge of Change: Engaging with God's Transformative Work

Transforming God, who is always at work within us, help us to accept the changes You are making in our lives. Give us the courage to let go of the old and to step into the new paths You are paving for us. Strengthen our faith as we trust in Your plans for transformation. Amen.

Scripture Reading:

Isaiah 43:19

"See, I am doing a new thing! Now it springs up; do you not perceive it? I am making a way in the wilderness and streams in the wasteland."

Reflection:

Change can often be daunting, even when we know it's for our growth and good. God's promise to do a new thing in our lives is both exhilarating and challenging. It requires us to trust in His vision, even when the path is unclear. Embracing change means letting go of our comfort zones and stepping out in faith, believing that God is leading us to a place of greater fruitfulness and fulfillment. This transformation process is how we grow more into the likeness of Christ, finding streams of living water in our wilderness.

Reflect on the areas of your life where God might be initiating change. What fears or hesitations do you have about stepping into this new thing God is doing? How can you cultivate a posture of openness and trust in God's transformative work?

Action Step:

Identify one specific change you feel God is calling you to make. Spend time in prayer, asking for the courage and faith to move forward. Consider sharing this step with a trusted friend or mentor who can offer support and accountability as you embrace God's transformative work in your life.

Lord of New Beginnings, we praise You for Your ongoing work of transformation in our lives. Guide us through the changes You are bringing, and help us to see the beauty and potential in what is to come. May we walk boldly in the new paths You are setting before us, trusting in Your goodness and faithfulness every step of the way. Amen.

Saturday, April 5

The Power of Prayerful Presence: Encountering God in Silence

Lord of Quiet, who speaks in the silence of our hearts, draw us into the power of Your prayerful presence. Teach us the value of stillness, where we can encounter You beyond words and busy thoughts. Amen.

Scripture Reading:

1 Kings 19:11-12

"And He said, 'Go out and stand on the mountain before the Lord.' And behold, the Lord passed by, and a great and strong wind tore the mountains and broke in pieces the rocks before the Lord, but the Lord was not in the wind. And after the wind an earthquake, but the Lord was not in the earthquake. And after the earthquake a fire, but the Lord was not in the fire. And after the fire the sound of a low whisper."

Reflection:

In a world that is constantly filled with noise and distraction, the invitation to encounter God in silence is both a challenge and a gift. Elijah's experience on the mountain reveals that God often chooses to speak in the quiet, in the gentle whisper that can only be heard when we are fully present and attentive. This prayerful presence invites us into a deeper relationship with God, where we learn to listen more than we speak, to be still more than we act, and to simply be with God in the moment.

Consider your own practices of prayer and silence. How often do you allow yourself to simply be in God's presence without agenda or words? What might you discover about God and yourself if you embraced silence more fully?

Action Step:

Commit to spending a set time in silence before God each day this week. Start with just a few minutes if silence is unfamiliar to you, gradually increasing the time as you grow more comfortable. Use this time not to speak or ask but to be in God's presence. Note any thoughts, feelings, or impressions that come to you during these times.

God of the Whisper, thank You for the invitation to encounter You in the silence. Help us to cultivate a practice of stillness where we can hear Your voice and know Your heart more deeply. May this time in Your presence refresh and renew us, drawing us closer to You each day. Amen.

Sunday, April 6

Reflecting Jesus's Heart: Compassion in Action

Loving God, who revealed Your heart through Jesus Christ, mold our hearts to reflect His compassion. Empower us to put love into action, showing the world the depth of Your care. Amen.

———◆○◆———

Scripture Reading:

Matthew 9:35-36

"Jesus went through all the towns and villages, teaching in their synagogues, proclaiming the good news of the kingdom and healing every disease and sickness. When he saw the crowds, he had compassion on them, because they were harassed and helpless, like sheep without a shepherd."

———◆○◆———

Reflection:

Jesus's ministry was marked by a deep, abiding compassion for people in all walks of life. His response to the crowds—harassed and helpless—was not one of judgment or indifference but of heartfelt compassion that moved Him to action. This same compassion is called to be the hallmark of our lives as followers of Christ. It challenges us to look beyond our own needs and comforts, to see the needs of those around us, and to be moved to action by love.

Reflect on how you can more fully embody Jesus's compassionate heart in your daily interactions. Are there specific individuals or groups in your community who are in need of compassion and care? How can you be an instrument of God's love to them?

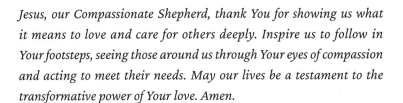

Action Step:

Choose one practical way this week to demonstrate compassion to someone in need. This could be volunteering your time, offering support to a friend or stranger, or advocating for a cause that addresses the needs of the vulnerable. Let your action reflect Jesus's love and compassion.

Jesus, our Compassionate Shepherd, thank You for showing us what it means to love and care for others deeply. Inspire us to follow in Your footsteps, seeing those around us through Your eyes of compassion and acting to meet their needs. May our lives be a testament to the transformative power of Your love. Amen.

Monday, April 7
The Harmony of Hope: Sustaining Faith in Difficult Times

God of Hope, in the midst of our trials and tribulations, tune our hearts to the harmony of Your hope. Let this hope sustain our faith, carrying us through difficult times with the assurance of Your presence and promises. Amen.

Scripture Reading:

Romans 15:13

"May the God of hope fill you with all joy and peace as you trust in Him, so that you may overflow with hope by the power of the Holy Spirit."

Reflection:

Hope is a melody that resonates within the believer's heart, a divine assurance that, despite life's discordant moments, there is a harmonious plan orchestrated by God. This hope is not passive; it is active and empowering, enabling us to face challenges with a sense of peace and joy that surpasses understanding.

The Holy Spirit within us tunes our hearts to this hope, reminding us of God's faithfulness and the eternal joy that awaits us.

Reflect on the current challenges in your life. How does the hope of God's presence and promises sustain you? How can you more fully embrace this hope to navigate difficult times?

Action Step:

Identify one area in your life where you need the sustenance of hope. Commit to a daily practice of meditating on a promise from Scripture that speaks to this need. Ask the Holy Spirit to fill you with hope, joy, and peace as you trust in God, and look for opportunities to share this hope with others who may be facing their own challenges.

Heavenly Father, thank You for the gift of hope that sustains us through every season of life. Fill us afresh with Your Spirit, that we may overflow with hope, radiating Your joy and peace to a world in need. Strengthen our faith to hold onto Your promises, confident in Your loving plan for our lives. Amen.

Tuesday, April 8
Courage to Confront: Standing Firm in Faith

God of Strength, who equips us with courage, embolden us to stand firm in our faith, confronting challenges and injustices with the confidence that comes from knowing You are with us. Grant us wisdom and discernment in our actions, reflecting Your love and truth in all we do. Amen.

Scripture Reading:

Ephesians 6:13

"Therefore put on the full armor of God, so that when the day of evil comes, you may be able to stand your ground, and after you have done everything, to stand."

Reflection:

To live out our faith in a world often opposed to the values of God's kingdom requires courage—a courage not born of our own strength but of the assurance that God is with us. The Apostle Paul's metaphor of the armor of God is a vivid reminder that we are engaged in a spiritual battle, one that demands our readiness and resilience. Standing firm in faith means confronting not just personal trials, but also societal injustices, armed with the truth, righteousness, peace, faith, and salvation offered to us in Christ.

Reflect on the areas of your life or the world around you where God calls you to stand firm and confront injustice. What does it mean for you to put on the full armor of God in these situations?

Action Step:

Identify one issue or situation where you feel called to take a stand for your faith or for justice. Pray for guidance on how to approach this challenge with courage and wisdom. Consider seeking support from your faith community or like-minded individuals who can stand with you in this effort.

Lord of Justice and Truth, thank You for the armor You provide us to face the battles before us. Help us to stand firm in our faith, courageously confronting the challenges and injustices of our time. May we do so with Your wisdom, strength, and love, serving as beacons of Your light in the darkness. In Jesus' name, we pray. Amen.

Wednesday, April 9
The Beauty of Creation: Witnessing God's Handiwork

Creator God, who fashioned the universe with Your word, open our eyes to the beauty of Your creation that surrounds us. Help us to see Your handiwork in the intricacies of nature, leading us to worship and wonder at Your creative power. Amen.

Scripture Reading:

Psalm 19:1

"The heavens declare the glory of God; the skies proclaim the work of His hands."

Reflection:

The beauty of creation is a testament to God's glory and creativity. Every mountain peak, every sunrise, and every blooming flower speaks of His majesty and care. In our busy lives, it's easy to overlook these daily miracles that reveal God's presence and His love for us. Taking time to witness and appreciate the beauty of creation deepens our relationship with God and nurtures a spirit of gratitude and stewardship for the world He has entrusted to us.

Reflect on your own experiences with nature. How have moments in the natural world drawn you closer to God? What can you do to more actively engage with and care for creation as a response to God's love?

Action Step:

Plan a time this week to intentionally engage with the beauty of creation. This could be as simple as a walk in a local park, a hike in the nearby hills, or even spending time in your garden. Use this time to reflect on God's creative power and offer gratitude prayers for the beauty surrounding you.

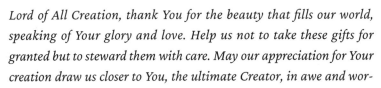

Lord of All Creation, thank You for the beauty that fills our world, speaking of Your glory and love. Help us not to take these gifts for granted but to steward them with care. May our appreciation for Your creation draw us closer to You, the ultimate Creator, in awe and worship. Amen.

Thursday, April 10
The Mystery of the Cross: Sharing in Our Suffering with Christ

Lord Jesus Christ, who bore our sins on the cross, help us to understand the depth of Your sacrifice and to find meaning in our suffering by uniting it with Yours. Grant us the grace to embrace our crosses with faith, seeing them as opportunities to grow closer to You. Amen.

Scripture Reading:

Philippians 3:10-11

"I want to know Christ—yes, to know the power of his resurrection and participation in his sufferings, becoming like him in his death, and so, somehow, attaining to the resurrection from the dead."

Reflection:

The cross stands as a paradoxical symbol of both suffering and victory. Christ's suffering on the cross was the ultimate act of love and redemption, offering us a path to eternal life. As followers of Christ, we are invited not only to rejoice in the Resurrection but also to share in His sufferings. This invitation challenges us to view our own trials and sufferings in light of the cross, finding in them a profound opportunity for union with Christ and spiritual growth.

Reflect on the sufferings you are currently experiencing or have faced. How can you offer them up in union with Christ's sufferings on the cross? How might this perspective transform your understanding of and approach to suffering?

Action Step:

Identify a current struggle or area of suffering in your life. Commit to a time of prayer where you specifically offer this suffering to God, asking Him to use it for your growth and to deepen your union with Christ. Consider writing down your reflections on this experience and any insights you gain through this process.

Merciful Savior, thank You for the gift of Your suffering on the cross, which brings us redemption and hope. Help us to accept our own sufferings with courage and faith, finding in them a deeper fellowship with You. May our trials refine us and lead us closer to the glory of Your Resurrection. Amen.

Friday, April 11
The Depth of Despair: Finding God in the Shadows

*Compassionate God, be our light in the shadows in times of despair.
Help us to find You even in the depths of our suffering, trusting that You
are with us, understanding our pain, and offering hope. Amen.*

Scripture Reading:

Psalm 34:18

"The Lord is close to the brokenhearted and saves those who are crushed in spirit."

Reflection:

Despair can feel like a deep, dark pit from which escape seems impossible. Yet, in these moments of our deepest pain, God's presence can be most profoundly felt. The Psalmist reminds us that God is especially close to the brokenhearted, offering salvation to those crushed in spirit. This divine closeness is a beacon of hope, a reminder that our suffering is not unnoticed and that God is actively involved in our healing and restoration.

Reflect on times when you have felt despair. How did you experience God's presence in those moments? What does it mean to you that God is close to the brokenhearted?

Action Step:

If you are currently experiencing a period of despair, take some time today to reach out to God in prayer, honestly sharing your feelings and fears. Alternatively, if you know someone who is going through a tough time, consider reaching out to them with a message of hope or an offer of support, embodying God's love and closeness.

Lord of Comfort and Hope, thank You for being our refuge in times of despair. Help us to always remember Your nearness in our darkest moments, and give us the strength to reach out to You. May we also be a source of comfort to others who are suffering, reflecting Your love and compassion. Amen.

Saturday, April 12
The Silence of Saturday: Waiting with Hope

Lord of Waiting, in the silence of Saturday, teach us the discipline of hopeful waiting. As we sit in the space between sorrow and joy, help us to trust in Your promises and to hold fast to the hope of Resurrection. Amen.

Scripture Reading:

Luke 23:55-56

"The women who had come with Jesus from Galilee followed Joseph and saw the tomb and how his body was laid in it. Then they went home and prepared spices and perfumes. But they rested on the Sabbath in obedience to the commandment."

Reflection:

The silence of Saturday represents a profound period of waiting—a time filled with sorrow, uncertainty, and yet, a glimmer of hope. It's a reminder of the times in our lives when God seems silent, when our situations appear hopeless, and yet, the promise of God's intervention lingers on the horizon. This day challenges us to hold onto faith even when the evidence of God's work is not yet visible and to rest in His promises despite our uncertainties.

Consider the "Saturdays" in your own life—times of waiting for God's intervention or deliverance. How do you hold onto hope in these periods of silence? How can the discipline of hopeful waiting strengthen your faith?

Action Step:

Reflect on a current situation in your life where you are in a period of waiting. Commit to praying, offering your worries and expectations to God, and asking for the patience and faith to wait on His timing. Consider writing a letter to God, expressing your trust in His plan and timing, even when the outcome is not yet known.

Heavenly Father, in the quiet of our waiting, fill us with the peace and hope that comes from trusting in You. Help us to remember the lessons of Saturday—that Your silence is not absence, and Your timing is perfect. May our hearts be steadfast in hope, anticipating the joy of Resurrection and Your fulfillment of all promises. Amen.

Holy Week: From Death to Resurrection

As we approach the threshold of Holy Week, we enter into the heart of the Christian narrative—a journey from death to Resurrection, from darkness into light. This sacred week invites us into a profound reflection on the passion, death, and Resurrection of Jesus Christ. It is a time to walk closely with Jesus, from the jubilant entry into Jerusalem on Palm Sunday to the solemnity of the Last Supper, the agony of Gethsemane, the desolation of Good Friday, and the silent waiting of Holy Saturday, culminating in the joyous celebration of Easter Sunday.

Palm Sunday marks the beginning of Holy Week, as we remember Jesus' triumphant entry into Jerusalem, welcomed with palms and shouts of "Hosanna!" Yet, this joy is tinged with the shadow of what is to come, a foreshadowing of the suffering and sacrifice that lies ahead.

Maundy Thursday invites us into the intimacy of the Last Supper, where Jesus, knowing the end is near, offers himself as bread and wine, establishing a new covenant of love and service. It's here Jesus washes his disciples' feet, a profound act of humility and a call for us to love and serve one another.

Good Friday plunges us into the depths of Jesus' suffering and death on the cross. It's a day of reflection on the cost of our redemption, the weight of sin, and the boundless love of God, who offers His only Son for the world's salvation. The cross symbolizes suffering and defeat and becomes the ultimate expression of divine love and forgiveness.

Holy Saturday is a day of quiet and waiting, a solemn vigil where the whole earth seems to hold its breath. It is a time to meditate on the mystery of Jesus' death and burial, sit in the tomb's silence, and wait in hope for the promise of Resurrection.

Easter Sunday breaks the silence with the joyous proclamation, "He is risen!" It is the pinnacle of the Christian faith, the glorious celebration of Jesus' victory over death, promising eternal life to all who believe. This day transforms all sorrow into joy, all despair into hope, affirming that love is stronger than death.

As we journey through Holy Week, we are reminded that this sacred narrative is not merely a historical recounting of events long past but a living reality that continues to unfold within and among us. Each step of this journey—from the jubilation of Palm Sunday to the somber reflection of Good Friday and the triumphant joy of Easter Sunday—invites us into a deeper relationship with Christ and with one another.

In the rhythms of Holy Week, we find the patterns of our own lives—moments of celebration and sorrow, times of waiting and moments of revelation. Here, in the confluence of divine mystery and human experience, we are called to a renewed commitment to live out the values of the Kingdom of God: love that knows no bounds, service that seeks no reward, and hope that transcends the darkest of circumstances.

Let us, therefore, emerge from Holy Week not as bystanders to a story of ages past but as participants in the ongoing story of God's redeeming love. May the profound truths we commemorate and celebrate during these holy days inspire us to live with greater faith, love, and courage. Let the memory of Christ's passion stir us to compassion for all who suffer. May the silence of Holy Saturday teach us to wait with patience and trust in God's timing. And let the joy of the Resurrection fill us with hope, propelling us forward to be bearers of light in a world that so desperately needs it.

As we close this chapter, may we carry the lessons of Holy Week into every aspect of our lives, letting them shape us, challenge us, and draw us ever closer to the heart of God. With hearts full of gratitude and mouths ready to proclaim, "He is risen indeed," let us walk in the newness of life that Christ has won for us, today and always. Amen.

Palm Sunday, April 13

Entering Jerusalem: A Journey of Faith and Fulfillment

Lord of All Journeys, as we reflect on Jesus' triumphant entry into Jerusalem, inspire us to walk our own paths of faith with courage and conviction. Guide us toward the fulfillment of Your will in our lives, as we seek to honor You in all we do. Amen.

Scripture Reading:

Matthew 21:1-11

"As they approached Jerusalem and came to Bethphage on the Mount of Olives, Jesus sent two disciples, saying to them, 'Go to the village ahead of you, and at once you will find a donkey tied there, with her colt by her. Untie them and bring them to me. If anyone says anything to you, say that the Lord needs them, and he will send them right away.' ... The crowds that went ahead of him and those that followed shouted, 'Hosanna to the Son of David! Blessed is he who comes in the name of the Lord! Hosanna in the highest heaven!'"

Reflection:

Jesus' entry into Jerusalem marks a pivotal moment in the journey of faith—not only for Christ but for all who follow Him. It is a declaration of kingship, a fulfillment of prophecy, and a bold step toward the ultimate sacrifice for humanity's redemption. This event invites us to consider our own journeys of faith. How do we respond to Jesus' call to follow Him, even when the path leads through trials and sacrifices? Are we prepared to lay down our own "cloaks" in recognition of His lordship over our lives?

Reflect on your journey of faith. What does it mean for you to welcome Jesus into the "Jerusalem" of your heart? How can you live out this welcome in your daily actions and decisions?

Action Step:

In the spirit of Palm Sunday, take some time to prayerfully commit or recommit your life to Jesus, acknowledging Him as Lord. Consider what practical steps you can take this week to demonstrate your faith and trust in Him. It might involve a specific act of service, a commitment to prayer, or sharing your faith journey with someone else.

King of Glory, we praise You for Your faithful journey to Jerusalem, a journey that led to our salvation. Help us to follow You with boldness and love, laying down our lives as a response to Your great sacrifice. May our lives reflect Your glory and grace, drawing others to our hope in You. Amen.

Monday, April 14

The Last Supper's Lesson: Unity and Sacrifice

Lord Jesus, as we remember the Last Supper, instill in us the profound lessons of unity and sacrifice You demonstrated. Help us to embody these principles in our lives, drawing closer to You and to one another in love and service. Amen.

Scripture Reading:

Luke 22:19-20

"And he took bread, gave thanks and broke it, and gave it to them, saying, 'This is my body given for you; do this in remembrance of me.' In the same way, after the supper he took the cup, saying, 'This cup is the new covenant in my blood, which is poured out for you.'"

Reflection:

The Last Supper, shared among Jesus and His disciples, is a moment of deep intimacy and profound instruction. It encapsulates the essence of Christ's mission—unity among His followers and the ultimate sacrifice of His life for the redemption of humanity. This meal is not just a historical event but a living invitation to participate in the life and love of Christ. It calls us to remember

His sacrifice, to live in unity with our brothers and sisters in Christ, and to be willing to lay down our lives for one another in love.

Reflect on how the principles of unity and sacrifice are manifested in your life. How can you more fully participate in the unity of the body of Christ? In what ways are you called to live out sacrificial love?

Action Step:

Consider participating in a communal meal with fellow believers, whether it's through a formal communion service at your church or a simple meal shared in remembrance of the Last Supper. Use this time to reflect on the unity and sacrifice that Jesus taught us, committing to live out these values in your relationships and community.

Jesus, our Bread of Life, thank You for the gift of the Last Supper and the lessons it teaches us. May we cherish the unity You've given us in Your body, the church, and be ever willing to offer ourselves in love and service, just as You did. Unite us in Your love, and help us to live out the covenant of Your sacrifice daily. Amen.

Tuesday, April 15
The Agony in the Garden: Surrendering to God's Will

Father of Comfort, who witnessed Your Son's agony in the garden, teach us the power of surrender to Your will, even in our most trying moments. Grant us the courage to say, "Not my will, but Yours be done," trusting in Your wisdom and love. Amen.

Scripture Reading:

Luke 22:41-42

"He withdrew about a stone's throw beyond them, knelt down and prayed, 'Father, if you are willing, take this cup from me; yet not my will, but yours be done.'"

Reflection:

In the quiet of Gethsemane, Jesus faced the full weight of what was to come—the suffering, the cross, the burden of humanity's sin. Yet, in this moment of profound agony, His prayer was one of ultimate surrender to the Father's will. This act of submission was not a sign of weakness but of immense strength and trust in God. It challenges us to consider our own response to God's will, especially when it leads us through paths of difficulty and suffering.

Reflect on areas of your life where you struggle to surrender to God's will. What fears or desires are holding you back from fully trusting in Him? How can Jesus' example in the garden inspire you to a deeper level of surrender and faith?

Action Step:

Identify a specific situation where you need to surrender to God's will more fully. Spend time in prayer, echoing Jesus' words in the garden, offering your desires, fears, and plans to God and asking for the strength to embrace His will, whatever it may be.

Lord Jesus, in Your agony, You showed us the way of surrender. Help us to follow Your example, laying down our wills before the Father, confident in His good and perfect plans for us. In moments of fear and uncertainty, remind us of Your faithful submission and the victory it brought. May we find peace and strength in surrender, trusting that Your grace is sufficient for us. Amen. Amen.

Wednesday, April 16
The Betrayal and Arrest: Facing Trials with Grace

Lord of Grace, who faced betrayal and arrest with unwavering love and dignity, help us to navigate our own trials with the same grace that You demonstrated. Strengthen us to stand firm in faith, offering forgiveness and love even in the face of betrayal. Amen.

⎯⎯⎯◇⎯⎯⎯

Scripture Reading:

Matthew 26:47-50

"While he was still speaking, Judas, one of the Twelve, arrived. With him was a large crowd armed with swords and clubs, sent from the chief priests and the elders of the people. Now the betrayer had arranged a signal with them: 'The one I kiss is the man; arrest him.' Going at once to Jesus, Judas said, 'Greetings, Rabbi!' and kissed him. Jesus replied, 'Do what you came for, friend.'"

⎯⎯⎯◇⎯⎯⎯

Reflection:

The betrayal and arrest of Jesus mark the beginning of the fulfillment of God's redemptive plan, yet they also reveal the depth of human frailty and sin. Jesus' response to Judas—not with anger or retaliation, but with a calm acknowledgment and the poignant address of "friend"—challenges us to consider how we face our own betrayals and trials. In moments of hurt and injustice, can we, like Jesus, respond with grace, forgiveness, and an unwavering commitment to God's will?

Reflect on your experiences of betrayal or injustice. How have you responded? How can you seek to embody Jesus' grace and forgiveness in similar situations?

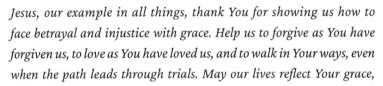

Action Step:

Consider a situation where you feel wronged or betrayed. Pray for the grace to forgive those involved and ask God for the strength to respond with love and dignity. If possible, take a tangible step toward reconciliation or forgiveness, trusting in God to heal and restore.

Jesus, our example in all things, thank You for showing us how to face betrayal and injustice with grace. Help us to forgive as You have forgiven us, to love as You have loved us, and to walk in Your ways, even when the path leads through trials. May our lives reflect Your grace, bringing glory to Your name. Amen.

Holy Thursday, April 17
The Trial and Denial: Standing Firm in Faith

Lord of Truth, who stood before Your accusers with integrity and silence, strengthen us to stand firm in our faith amidst trials and denials. Help us to remain faithful to You, even when faced with the temptation to deny our allegiance to Your truth. Amen.

Scripture Reading:

Mark 14:53-54, 66-72

"They took Jesus to the high priest, and all the chief priests, the elders and the teachers of the law came together. ... Peter followed him at a distance, right into the courtyard of the high priest. There he sat with the guards and warmed himself at the fire. ... While Peter was below in the courtyard, one of the servant girls of the high priest came by. When she saw Peter warming himself, she looked closely at him. 'You also were with that Nazarene, Jesus,' she said. But he denied it. ... After a little while, those standing near said to Peter, 'Surely you are one of them, for you are a Galilean.' He began to call down curses, and he swore to them, 'I don't know this man you're talking about.'"

Reflection:

The trial of Jesus and Peter's subsequent denials highlight the stark contrast between human frailty and divine steadfastness. Jesus, in the face of false accusations and impending death, remained unwavering in His commitment to God's plan. Despite his earlier declarations of loyalty, Peter succumbed to fear and denied knowing Christ. This narrative invites us to examine our own faithfulness. Are we prepared to stand firm in our faith under pressure, or do we deny Christ, explicitly or through our actions and choices?

Reflect on your moments of trial or fear. Have there been times when you've failed to stand up for your faith? What can you learn from Jesus' example of integrity and Peter's journey of redemption?

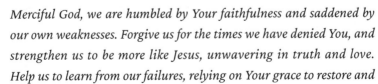

Action Step:

Identify areas in your life where you may be compromising or denying your faith due to fear or peer pressure. Commit to one specific action this week that demonstrates your faith publicly or reinforces your commitment to Christ. Seek God's forgiveness for past denials and ask for the courage to stand firm in the future.

Merciful God, we are humbled by Your faithfulness and saddened by our own weaknesses. Forgive us for the times we have denied You, and strengthen us to be more like Jesus, unwavering in truth and love. Help us to learn from our failures, relying on Your grace to restore and empower us. In Jesus' name, we pray. Amen.

Good Friday, April 18
The Crucifixion: Love's Ultimate Sacrifice

Lord Jesus, as we contemplate the profound mystery of the crucifixion, open our hearts to the depth of Your love and the magnitude of Your sacrifice. Help us to grasp even a fraction of what You endured for our sake, that we might live lives worthy of such a gift. Amen.

Scripture Reading:

John 19:16-18, 28-30

"Finally Pilate handed him over to them to be crucified. So the soldiers took charge of Jesus. Carrying his own cross, he went out to the place of the Skull (which in Aramaic is called Golgotha). There they crucified him, and with him two others—one on each side and Jesus in the middle. ... Later, knowing that everything had now been finished, and so that Scripture would be fulfilled, Jesus said, 'I am thirsty.' A jar of wine vinegar was there, so they soaked a sponge in it, put the sponge on a stalk of the hyssop plant, and lifted it to Jesus' lips. When he had received the drink, Jesus said, 'It is finished.' With that, he bowed his head and gave up his spirit."

Reflection:

The crucifixion of Jesus Christ stands as the central event in the Christian faith, a moment where love and suffering collide with redemptive power. It represents the ultimate expression of God's love for humanity—the willingness of Jesus to endure the cross, bearing the weight of our sins, to offer us forgiveness and eternal life. This sacrifice calls us to respond with gratitude, humility, and a deep commitment to living out this love in our own lives.

Reflect on the significance of the crucifixion in your personal faith journey. How does the reality of Jesus' sacrifice influence your understanding of love, forgiveness, and sacrifice? How are you called to embody this love in your interactions and decisions?

Action Step:

In response to contemplating the crucifixion, commit to a specific act of love or service this week that reflects Jesus' sacrificial love. It could be reaching out to someone in need, offering forgiveness where there has been hurt, or giving of your time and resources to serve others.

Jesus, our Savior, thank You for the unfathomable love displayed on the cross. May we never take for granted the price You paid for our freedom. Instill in us a profound sense of gratitude and responsibility to live out this love, sharing the message of the cross with the world around us. In Your holy name, we pray. Amen.

Saturday, April 19
The Tomb's Silence: A Time for Reflection and Hope

God of Mystery, in the silence of the tomb, teach us the value of reflection and the virtue of hope. As we await the joy of Resurrection, help us to ponder deeply the significance of Christ's death and anticipate the promise of new life with confidence. Amen.

Scripture Reading:

Matthew 27:57-60

"As evening approached, there came a rich man from Arimathea, named Joseph, who had himself become a disciple of Jesus. Going to Pilate, he asked for Jesus' body, and Pilate ordered that it be given to him. Joseph took the body, wrapped it in a clean linen cloth, and placed it in his own new tomb that he had cut out of the rock. He rolled a big stone in front of the entrance to the tomb and went away."

Reflection:

The silence of the tomb on the day after Jesus' crucifixion is a profound pause in the narrative of salvation, a moment laden with sorrow but also with hope. This pause invites us to reflect on the cost of our redemption and to prepare our hearts for the joy of Resurrection. It is a time to mourn what was lost but also to anticipate what is to come, recognizing that God's plans are always moving toward life, even when all seems lost.

Consider what the silence of the tomb symbolizes for you. How can you use times of waiting and uncertainty in your own life as opportunities for reflection and growth in hope?

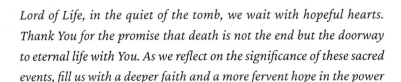

Action Step:

Set aside a quiet time to reflect on the events leading up to and including Jesus' burial. Consider writing in a journal or simply praying meditatively about these events. Contemplate the themes of sacrifice, love, and the hope of Resurrection. Ask God to deepen your understanding and appreciation of these truths.

Lord of Life, in the quiet of the tomb, we wait with hopeful hearts. Thank You for the promise that death is not the end but the doorway to eternal life with You. As we reflect on the significance of these sacred events, fill us with a deeper faith and a more fervent hope in the power of Your Resurrection. In Jesus' name, we pray. Amen.

Easter Sunday, April 20

Resurrection: Joy Comes in the Morning

Risen Lord, on this glorious day, we celebrate Your victory over death and the grave. Your Resurrection brings us joy, hope, and the promise of eternal life. Fill our hearts with the light of Your love, that we may live in the power of Your Resurrection every day. Amen.

———◆———

Scripture Reading:

Luke 24:1-6

"On the first day of the week, very early in the morning, the women took the spices they had prepared and went to the tomb. They found the stone rolled away from the tomb, but when they entered, they did not find the body of the Lord Jesus. While they were wondering about this, suddenly two men in clothes that gleamed like lightning stood beside them. In their fright the women bowed down with their faces to the ground, but the men said to them, 'Why do you look for the living among the dead? He is not here; he has risen! Remember how he told you, while he was still with you in Galilee.'"

———◆———

Reflection:

The Resurrection of Jesus Christ is the cornerstone of our faith, the triumphant declaration that death has been defeated and eternal life is available to all who believe in Him. This miraculous event shifts the narrative from despair to hope, from sorrow to joy, and from death to life. It invites us to live not as people of the tomb, but as people of the Resurrection—empowered by the Holy Spirit, living in freedom, and spreading the good news of Jesus Christ to the world.

Reflect on what the Resurrection means for you personally. How does it change the way you view life, death, and your daily walk with God? How can you embody the joy and hope of the Resurrection in your interactions and decisions?

Action Step:

Celebrate the Resurrection today in a way that is meaningful to you. This could be attending a worship service, sharing the story of Easter with someone who hasn't heard it, or spending time in nature reflecting on the new life all around. Let the reality of the Resurrection fill you with joy and propel you into action, living out the hope of Easter in every aspect of your life.

Heavenly Father, thank You for the gift of Your Son, Jesus, whose Resurrection has given us new life and hope. May the joy of this day renew our spirits and invigorate our faith. Help us to live as resurrection people, sharing the good news of Your love and the promise of eternal life with all we meet. In the name of the Risen Christ, we pray. Amen.

Conclusion

As we draw this Lenten journey to a close, I find myself reflecting on the profound path we have walked together. From the ashes of Ash Wednesday to the glorious dawn of Easter morning, we have ventured through a season of deep reflection, prayer, fasting, and almsgiving. It has been a time of facing our own wilderness, of embracing the disciplines that draw us closer to God, and of recognizing the boundless grace that sustains us.

Throughout these forty days, we've encountered challenges that tested our commitment and moments of grace that lifted our spirits. Each step has been an invitation to deeper communion with God, to see our lives through the lens of His love and sacrifice. This journey has not just been about the practices we've adopted but about the transformation happening within us—shaping us to be more reflective of Christ's love and compassion in our daily lives.

Now, as we stand on the threshold of Easter, I encourage you to carry the essence of Lent with you. Let the insights gained and the growth experienced not be confined to this season but continue to influence how you live and interact with the world around you. May the discipline of prayer, the simplicity learned in fasting, and the joy found in giving generously become woven into the fabric of your daily life.

I hope that this time has been as meaningful for you as it has been for me. My prayer for each of us is that we do not leave this season unchanged but that we move forward with hearts more attuned to God's voice and lives that more fully reflect His love. May the journey from death to resurrection we've commemorated inspire us to live with renewed hope, courage, and love.

As we part ways in this book, but not in spirit, I am grateful for your companionship on this sacred path. May God's grace continue to guide your steps, His peace fill your hearts, and His love inspire your actions. Until we meet again on these pages or in the communion of our shared faith, let us go forth in the joy of the Risen Christ, ready to embrace whatever lies ahead with open hearts and willing spirits.

Amen.

Dear reader,

Thank you for walking with me through the reflective season of Lent. I hope "The 2025 Lenten Companion" has been a beacon of spiritual insight and solace, guiding you closer to the heart of God and deepening your understanding of this sacred time.

If this book has enriched your Lenten journey, I would be deeply appreciative if you could share your experience with a review on Amazon. Your reflections are invaluable, helping others discover the transformative power of Lent and its capacity to renew and strengthen our faith. Posting a review is a meaningful way to support both my work and the spiritual journey of fellow believers.

May your path be illuminated with the light of Christ's love and resurrection.

With sincere gratitude,

Thomas Knight

My Notes

My Notes

My Notes

Made in the USA
Coppell, TX
27 February 2025

46504153R00070